Dedicated to my children, Matthew and Claire,
husband Larry, sponsor Susan,
and the Countless Others
who loved me when I could not love myself.

The Dragon Who Lives at Our House
Written by: Elaine Mitchell Palmore
Illustrated by: Norris Hall
Text and art copyright © 2011 by Elaine Mitchell Palmore

All rights reserved. No portion of this book may be reproduced in any form without the written permission of the publisher, with the exception of brief excerpts in reviews.
Published in Minneapolis, MN by Rising Star Studios, LLC.

Printed in the U.S.A.
P2_0112

Publisher's Cataloging-In-Publication Data
(Prepared by The Donohue Group, Inc.)

Palmore, Elaine Mitchell.
  The dragon who lives at our house / by Elaine Mitchell Palmore ; illustrated by Norris Hall.

    p. : chiefly col. ill. ; cm. -- (Fresh fables ; bk.1)

  When Al first came home with Dad, he was harmless and fun, but it soon became apparent that what seemed like fun could quickly get out of control. This story is a help to anyone trying to understand or discuss the heartbreak an hope of a family dealing with substance abuse or any life-controlling issue.
   Interest age group: 009-011.
   ISBN: 978-1-936086-95-5 (hardcover)
   ISBN: 978-1-936086-96-2 (pbk.)

   1. Dragons--Juvenile fiction. 2. Family crises--Juvenile fiction. 3. Father and child--Juvenile fiction. 4. Fathers--Substance use--Juvenile fiction. 5. Families--Psychological aspects--Juvenile fiction. 6. Dragons--Fiction. 7. Family problems--Fiction. 8. Father and child--Fiction. 9. Family life--Fiction. I. Hall, Norris (Norris M.), 1953- II. Title.

PZ7.P3566 Dr 2011
  [Fic]   2011922415

The Dragon Who Lives at Our House

fresh fables

A story of what it feels like to lose control of your life

BY ELAINE MITCHELL PALMORE
ILLUSTRATED BY NORRIS HALL

RISING STAR STUDIOS
MINNEAPOLIS, MN

There is a dragon at our house.

His name is Al.

It was not long before Al and my Dad became great friends.

Al was at our house more often and even went to work with Dad.

My Dad and Al made us all laugh.

My Mom called the way Dad and Al acted "antics."

Al made Dad feel happy.

After a while, Al grew bigger and moved into our house.

We began to see the "antics" and my coach asked them both to leave.

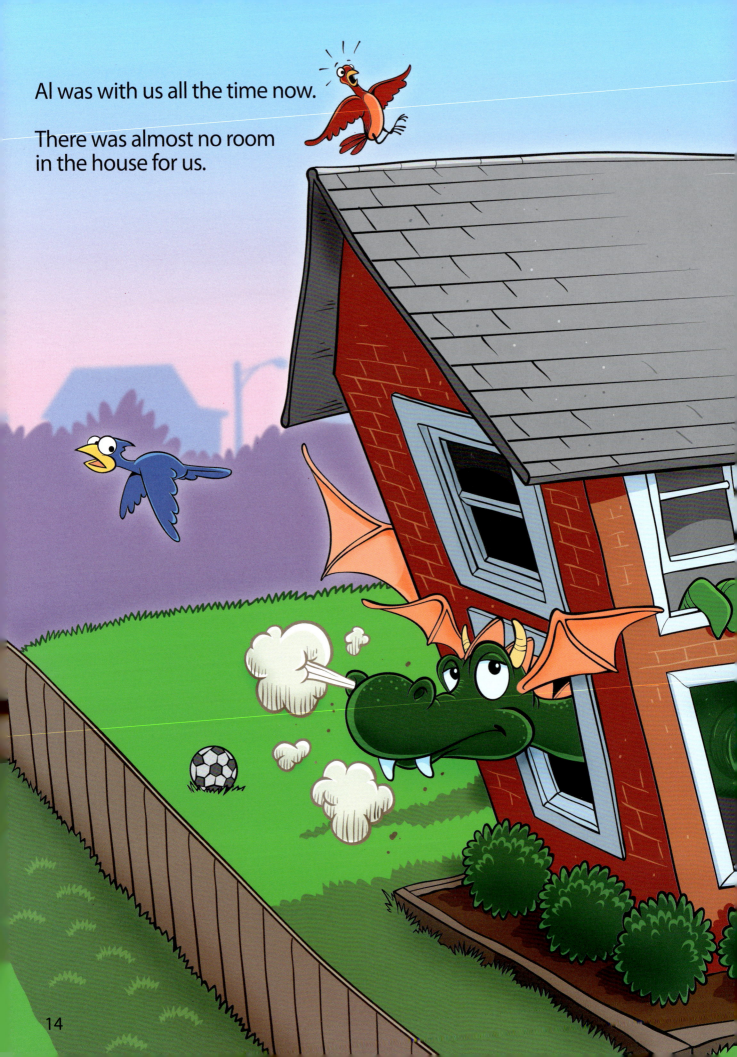

Al was with us all the time now.

There was almost no room in the house for us.

Mom told us at dinner last night that even though Dad is with Al most of the time he still loves us.

Mom has a plan for the times when Dad and Al get too rowdy.

We go to the neighbor's house or to our Granny's house far away.

This morning, Mom made an announcement: **ENOUGH!**

Phone calls were made.

In the afternoon some men came to talk to Dad and Al. They had dragons, too. The men asked Dad and Al to come with them to a place called "Treatment."

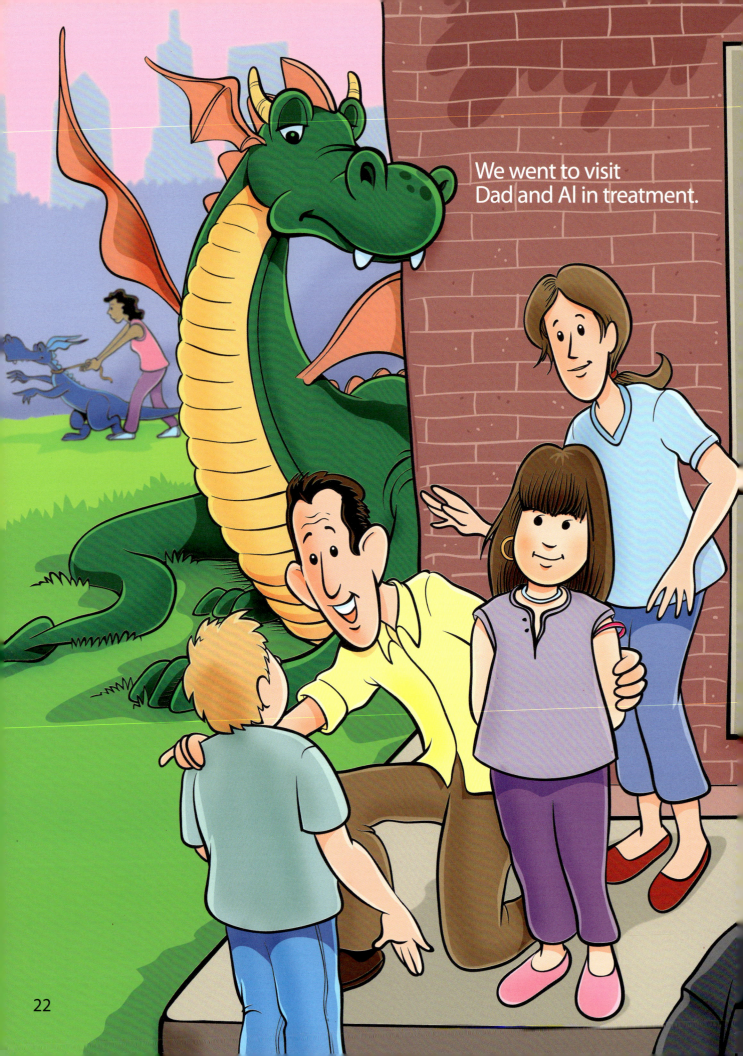

Dad explained to us that
Al the Dragon will always be with us.

He says he has to work a few simple steps to make sure Al doesn't take over our lives again.

Dad's new best friend is his sponsor. The sponsor has a dragon, too.

Afterword

As you read this book with/to someone who has been affected by a situation like the one depicted in The Dragon Who Lives at Our House, there will probably be feelings of abandonment, anger, confusion, frustration, and grief, perhaps with a large dose of self-pity thrown into the mix. There will also be the ever-present questions of: Why me? Why can't they stop? Why do they continue to embarrass me and themselves? Why can't we be like other families? This book was not written to solve any of these issues; it was written to open up a dialogue.

There is a solution, but not one solution that will fit everyone's needs. I do not know what the solution is for you, but what I do know is it is very important to not go through this alone. I encourage you to share your story with a trusted friend, counselor or anyone with whom you feel safe. You will soon discover there are so many others who have gone through a similar situation and there is so much wonderful help available. We have resources listed which may create a starting point for you, your family or any other person who can identify with these types of issues. Please use these resources with our blessings and know that there is hope.

-Elaine Mitchell Palmore

To view these resources visit
www.freshfables.com